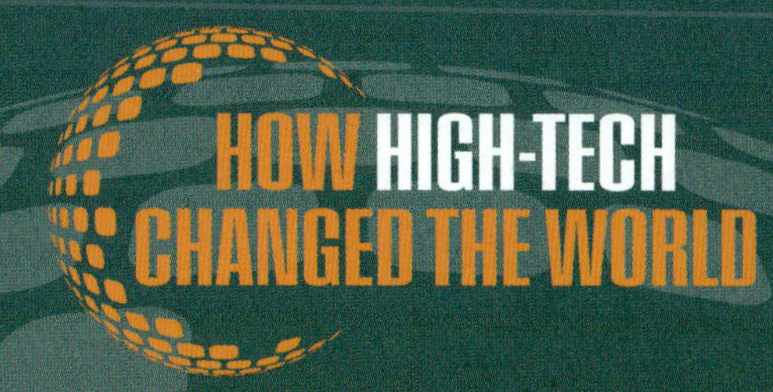

TOUCH SCREENS

Published in 2025 by **Cheriton Children's Books**
1 Bank Drive West, Shrewsbury, Shropshire, SY3 9DJ

© Copyright 2025 Cheriton Children's Books

First Edition

Author: Kelly Roberts
Designer: Paul Myerscough
Editor: Jennifer Sanderson
Proofreader: Amy Strauss
Consultant: David Hawksett, BSc

Picture credits: Cover: Shutterstock/Andrey Popov (t), Shutterstock/SkyNext (l), Shutterstock/Speed Stock (r), Shutterstock/Monkey Business Images (b). Inside: p4: Shutterstock/GaudiLab, p5: Shutterstock/Cast Of Thousands, p6: Shutterstock/Supakitswn, p7: Shutterstock/Andrey Popov, p8: Shutterstock/Grinny, p9: Shutterstock/Andrey Popov, p10: Shutterstock/Una Shimpraga, p11: Shutterstock/SkyNext, p12: Shutterstock/Anton27, p13: Shutterstock/Lomb, p14: Shutterstock/Bragin Alexey, p15: Shutterstock/Pressmaster, p16b: Wikimedia Commons/Sophia Elizabeth Bennett, p16t: Shutterstock/SrideeStudio, p17: Wikimedia Commons/GeneMosher, p18: Shutterstock/David Prado Perucha, p19b: Flickr/OnInnovation, p19t: Shutterstock/Monkey Business Images, p20: Shutterstock/Zern Liew, p21: Shutterstock/Andrey Popov, p22: Shutterstock/ESB Professional, p23: Shutterstock/Gorodenkoff, p24: Shutterstock/Lukmanazis, p25: Shutterstock/Twin Design, p26: Shutterstock/Kaspars Grinvalds, p27b: Shutterstock/PeopleImages.com/Yuri A, p27t: Wikimedia Commons/Alex Handy, p28: Shutterstock/Monkey Business Images, p29: Shutterstock/Sorbis, p30: Shutterstock/Fizkes, p31: Shutterstock/Kung Tom, p32: Shutterstock/OlegDoroshin, p33b: Wikimedia Commons/Evan Amos, p33t: Shutterstock/Chubykin Arkady, p34: Shutterstock/Josep Suria, p35: Shutterstock/NYCStock, p36: Shutterstock/PeopleImages.com/Yuri A, p37: Shutterstock/Stock 4you, p38: Shutterstock/Pramata, p39b: Wikimedia Commons/Felix Winkelnkemper, p39t: Shutterstock/Mhong84, p40: Shutterstock/Rokas Tenys, p41: Shutterstock/David Gyung, p42: Shutterstock/Mario Hagen, p43: Shutterstock/Framesira, p44: Shutterstock/Rawpixel.com, p45: Shutterstock/Thinkhubstudio.

All rights reserved. No part of this book may be reproduced in any form without permission of the publisher, except by a reviewer.

Printed in China

Please visit our website,
www.cheritonchildrensbooks.com
to see more of our high-quality books.

CONTENTS

CHAPTER 1

THE TOUCH SCREEN STORY

Touch screens are visual displays that people use to control a range of electronic gadgets, from game consoles and tablet computers to smartphones and satellite navigation (sat-nav) systems. Most touch screen devices work by sensing the movement of the user's fingers on a flat screen. As the user swipes or taps the screen, the computer turns these finger movements into commands. These commands control icons on the screen. For example, a tap on the screen might click on an icon, and a swipe might zoom in on an object on the screen.

What Came Before

Before the touch screen there was the light pen. This input device was invented in the early 1950s. It worked by detecting the brightness of pixels on the screen and so allowing a computer to determine exactly what the pen was touching. The light pen allowed users to draw on the screen. They were common in the 1970s and 1980s but have now mostly been replaced by touch screens.

Touch screens have made our lives easier. Buying train tickets and ordering food using a touch screen interface can help us to avoid standing in a line.

Some touch screen devices work by using a pen-shaped stylus or digital pen to control the device. These tools work in exactly the same way as your fingers—they input commands by tapping and drawing on the screen of the device.

Not-So-New Tech

Most people think that the touch screen is a modern technology. In fact, the first touch screen was invented in 1965. British engineer Eric Johnson was working at the Royal Radar Establishment when he described his invention as a "novel input/output device for computers."

Touch Screens Today

Today, touch screens are common in many everyday electronic devices. In this book we'll discover more about the technology that makes touch screens work. We'll also explore the history of touch screens, how they have changed your world, and the brilliant scientists behind this incredible invention.

HOW HIGH-TECH CHANGED THE WORLD

Touch screens have changed the way people use electronic equipment. They make using devices much easier because you can control the computer directly on the display. Instead of using buttons, a mouse, or a keyboard, you can simply touch, tap, and swipe the screen. We can now control a lot of our lives simply by touching a screen.

Touch Screen Tech

Most people take touch screens for granted when they use smartphones, tablets, and other electronic devices. However, touch screens are packed with a lot of amazing technology. Some devices use resistive touch screens to sense touch. Resistive touch screens consist of a flat glass surface coated with two main layers. One layer is made up of a conductive material, which conducts electricity very well. The second layer consists of a resistive material, which does not conduct electricity as well. Spacers between the conductive and resistive layers separate them so that they do not touch.

Touching the Screen

When you switch on a device that has a resistive touch screen, electricity flows through the conductive and resistive layers. Since the two layers are separate, nothing happens. However, when you use your finger or a stylus to put pressure on the screen, the two layers make contact. The computer in the device measures the change in electricity at the contact point. This tells the computer to make something happen—for example, to open an app.

Entertainment on a commercial jet consists of a touch screen and headset. Each passenger can choose to play games or watch television and movies.

Pressing Hard Works

Resistive touch screens work under pressure from almost any hard object. You can use your finger or a stylus to control the device as long as you press hard enough on the screen. Since the conductive and resistive layers pinpoint the exact contact point, resistive touch screens are very accurate. However, they do not respond to light touches.

The part of the screen you touch to control the device is usually a flat glass or plastic surface. This part of the touch screen device is covered with a scratch-resistant substance to prevent the screen from being damaged.

HIGH-TECH STARS WHO CHANGED THE WORLD

GEORGE SAMUEL HURST

In 1971, George Samuel Hurst (1927–2010) at the University of Kentucky led the team that created the first resistive touch screen. The team was studying atomic physics and Hurst and his colleagues realized they could use special paper that conducted electricity to speed up their analyses. They knew their invention could have other uses so they created a prototype for a computer touch screen. The university believed that the screen would be useful only to scientific research but the team knew better! This new type of screen was much cheaper to make than the existing ones and soon became the most popular type of touch screen.

It's All about Electricity

Did you know that some touch screens actually transfer electricity to your fingers when you touch them? These touch screens are called capacitive touch screens. They work by storing and releasing electrical charges. Capacitive touch screens work only using finger touch. You cannot use a stylus on a capacitive screen because the stylus cannot pick up electrical charge from the screen.

A Drop in Charge

The device measures the drop in electrical charge using four electronic circuits—one at each corner of the screen. The computer in the touch screen device figures out the difference in electrical charge at each corner. It then uses this information to calculate exactly where the user's finger touched the screen. Just like the resistive touch screen, a capacitive touch screen measures the change in electrical charge at the contact point to make something happen, such as swiping the screen to move to a new page.

Keeping up to Date

When adding a new external device to a personal computer (PC), such as a printer or gaming steering wheel, new drivers for these need to be installed. Similarly, every touch screen device has a computer program called a touch screen driver. The driver is computer code that translates the information from the touch screen into a command that the computer can understand. This command tells the computer what to do. Manufacturers regularly improve their drivers and the device will usually alert its owner that the latest version is available to download, keeping the device up to date with the latest technology.

Capacitive touch screens used in smart phones are very sensitive. You can swipe across the screen with the lightest touch to get a response. The down side of capacitive touch screens is that they are less precise than other types of touch screen.

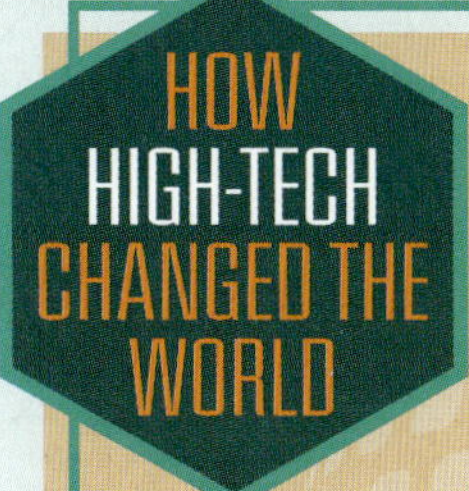

Today, adding an external touch screen to a computer is easy but it was less simple before the mid-1990s. Back then it meant reading the PC's manual and, in the case of hard drives, physically selecting tiny switches on the drive so the PC knew what kind of storage it was to be used for. Many people would pay a computer expert to do this for them. When Microsoft launched Windows 95, the operating system could recognize any device plugged in the appropriate socket. This advancement created a boom in the development of computer input and output devices.

A keyboard is a common input device and a normal screen is an output device. Touch screens are both input and output devices. A touch screen personal device can often also be controlled by more traditional input devices, such as a wireless keyboard and mouse.

Screens That Use Sound

Some touch screens work by using sound waves that flow across the surface of the glass display. These touch screens are called surface acoustic wave (SAW) touch screens, and they work by using an electronic part called a transducer. A transducer changes energy from one form into another. When you switch on a SAW touch screen device, the transducer changes electrical power from the device into sound energy. This sound energy then travels across the surface of the glass as sound waves.

Receiving a Signal

SAW touch screen devices contain two transducers. One of these transducers is a transmitting transducer. It sends the sound signals across the glass screen of the device. The second transducer is the receiving transducer. This transducer detects these sound waves and converts them back into electrical signals. SAW touch screens also have reflectors lined up along the edge of the glass display. They reflect the sound signal from the transmitting transducer onto the receiving transducer.

Disturbing the Waves

When someone touches the surface of a SAW touch screen, they absorb some of the sound waves flowing across the glass screen. The receiving transducer registers this change to find the touching point on the screen. This sends a command to the computer in the touch screen device to tell it what to do.

SAW touch screens are ideal for busy places with bright lighting, such as shopping malls, where they are used for automated teller machines (ATMs).

Saw touch screens are often used in self-service kiosks because of their simplicity and durability.

Top Quality

SAW touch screens have very good image quality partly because they do not need to have an additional layer between the user and the screen itself. This means they can be used in brightly lit places and they can be used with a finger, stylus, or a finger in a glove. They need to be kept clean as any dirt on the screen can disrupt the ultrasonic waves and reduce their accuracy. SAW touch screens need to be very tough, as a scratch can make a "dead spot" where a touch is not properly detected.

HIGH-TECH HISTORY

SAW touch screens became popular in the early 1990s in busy places where a lot of people need to get information. These included airports, shopping malls, and museums. By the early 2000s, before people had smartphones, many SAW touch screens were connected to the Internet and could offer online services as well as local information.

Using Little Lights

Some touch screen devices work using a grid of infrared light. The infrared light is created by electronic parts called light-emitting diodes (LEDs). LEDs are like tiny lightbulbs that light up to provide a source of light. Light-emitting diodes are widely used in electronic equipment to do many different tasks. They are often used as flashing warning lights in alarm systems, but they can also be found in flashlights and traffic lights. LEDs last much longer than normal lightbulbs and they are small enough to fit in tiny electrical circuits. This makes them perfect for use in touch screen devices.

LED TVs and monitors use tiny light-emitting diodes to create moving or still images. This technology has allowed screens to become larger and thinner.

On the Grid

The LEDs in some types of touch screen device work using infrared light. They are placed along two adjoining sides of the screen. This creates a grid of light across the display. Light detectors on the opposite edges of the screen pick up the light beams as they travel across the surface of the glass.

Interrupting the Grid

When someone touches the screen of a touch screen device fitted with LEDs, the light grid is disturbed. The light detectors register the change in the light signal to figure out the touching point on the screen. This feeds back to the touch screen driver to give the computer a command, telling it what to do.

Smartphones and their apps use simple graphical interfaces designed to be used with fingers, or even one-handed using just one thumb.

HIGH-TECH HISTORY

The first LED was created in 1927 by Russian inventor Oleg Losev (1903–1942). However, it did not produce light efficiently and it was decades before the LED had any practical use. In 1962, the first LED that could emit red light was invented and by the end of the 1970s, green LEDs had been invented. Ultra-bright blue LEDS were invented in 1994, which were soon modified to emit bright white light, paving the way for LED lighting to become common. LED lights are more environmentally friendly than older filament bulbs because they use far less electricity to produce the same amount of light.

Touch screens have changed the way that we look at exhibits. Extra information, close-up images, and even three-dimensional (3-D) models can be accessed.

Little Cameras

Optical touch screens are a new development in touch screen technology. These touch screens use tiny cameras around two corners of the screen. The cameras detect objects moving close to the surface of the display. Optical touch screens can be either "active" or "passive." In active optical touch screens, the cameras placed around the touch screen point at a light source. This is usually an infrared LED (see pages 12–13). In passive optical touch screens, the cameras detect light bouncing off a special reflective surface on the other side of the screen.

Commands and Shadows

When someone uses an optical touch screen, the cameras detect the change in light across the screen to figure out the touching point. This feeds back to the touch screen driver to give the device's computer a command to do something. The real advantage of optical touch screens is that they can detect a "touch" without the user actually making contact with the screen. This works because the cameras pick up shadows of objects, such as the user's finger, moving near the display.

Too Much Light

One of the main problems with optical touch screens is that normal background light can stop them from working properly. In bright sunlight, for example, the cameras may not detect light from the LED light source, and the touch screen can fail.

HOW HIGH-TECH CHANGED THE WORLD

Most touch screens have a liquid-crystal display (LCD). Liquid crystals are a type of matter that have some properties of both liquids and solids. Inventor and engineer George Heilmeier (1936–2014) led the team that discovered a way to make liquid crystal change from transparent to opaque by applying a small electric current. In the 1960s, the team was working on a way to replace the cathode-ray tubes that were the technology behind all screens at the time. Their discovery led to the creation of the first LCD screen, without which there would be no touch screens today.

Early LCD screens were monochome (black and white), and these can still be found in devices such as calculators and digital watches.

CHAPTER 2

TOUCH SCREEN TECH IMPROVES

Most early touch screen devices were developed for special uses such as nuclear research and air traffic control. Over time, touch screens became easier and cheaper to build. Very quickly they started to appear in a huge range of everyday items such as cash registers, game consoles, PCs, and smartphones.

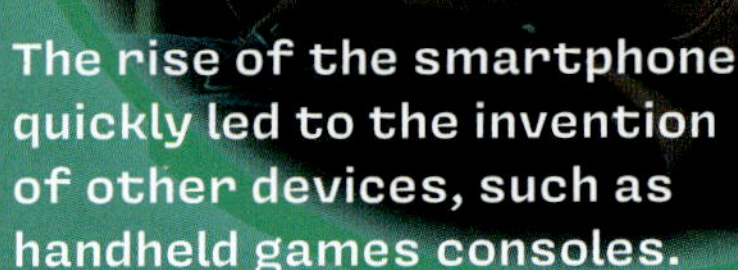

The rise of the smartphone quickly led to the invention of other devices, such as handheld games consoles.

Touch Screens Start

The touch screens that people use each day developed from research carried out by scientists and inventors in the late 1960s. In the early 1970s, Bent Stumpe and Frank Beck (1930–2020) —two engineers at CERN in Switzerland—designed one of the first touch screen devices. By 1973, CERN had manufactured and begun using their first touch screen computer.

Bent Stumpe shows a prototype for his capacitive touch screen along with a smartphone, the first invention that put touch screens in the hands of the general public.

No More Knobs and Buttons

Stumpe and Beck's touch screen computer was used to control a particle accelerator, which is a machine used to study atoms—the tiny particles that make up matter. Before the invention of the touch screen, the scientists operated the particle accelerator using thousands of buttons, knobs, and switches. The touch screen computer made controlling the particle accelerator much simpler, using fewer buttons on an easy-to-use screen. The CERN touch screen was a huge success and was used for more than 20 years.

Touch Screens in Cars

Soon, other industries started to look at touch screen technology. In the early 1980s, General Motors built the Electronic Control Center (ECC). The company designed the ECC with a touch screen so drivers could control systems such as air conditioning and heating in cars. The ECC met with little success, however, because the cost of repairs were far too high.

HIGH-TECH STARS WHO CHANGED THE WORLD

GENE MOSHER

An inventor named Gene Mosher demonstrated the first touch screen cash register, called ViewTouch, in 1986. It had a color screen and was powered by an Atari ST, which was launched in 1985, and which Mosher described as the only home computer that was "up to the job." It was first used in a restaurant in Springfield, Oregon. His invention became a commercial success. Today, most cash registers work using similar touch screen technology (see pages 28–29).

Touch screens in airports mean people can check-in or even buy their tickets using computer terminals. That saves people valuable time when traveling.

Protected by Patents

The first touch screen devices were at the cutting edge of science and technology, so researchers and inventors protected their products with patents. When an inventor comes up with an idea for a new product, they can protect the invention with a legal document, called a patent. A patent covers everything about the product, from how it works to how it is manufactured. Once an invention is protected by a patent, other people cannot copy the idea and only those with the patent are allowed to make and sell the invention around the world.

No Longer Under Patent

When touch screens were first developed, inventors took out patents to protect their products. But most of these patents ran out at the start of the twenty-first century. This meant that anyone with the technological know-how could develop touch screens. So, touch screen technology developed very quickly. And as a result, touch screens have become part of many everyday electronic gadgets.

Many students use tablet computers. They are small enough to be carried and worked on almost anywhere.

Cheaper and Cheaper

One of the biggest problems with early touch screen devices was their cost to build, which made them expensive to own. The first touch screens used up a lot of computer power, which was extremely expensive. Computer power is much cheaper today, so the cost of making touch screen devices has fallen to make the technology more accessible to more people.

HIGH-TECH STARS WHO CHANGED THE WORLD

GORDON MOORE

Gordon Moore (1929–2023) was the cofounder of the Intel Corporation, the microprocessor manufacturer. A microprocessor is the "brain of the computer." It is a device built on a microchip or integrated circuit (IC) that processes all the information in a computer. In 1965, Moore stated that the number of transistors on a microchip doubles around every two years, and that this leads to the doubling of computer power each time. This has become known as "Moore's Law." The increase in computer power and miniaturization has enabled modern computers to be fully contained behind a touch screen. This includes not only tablets but also "panel PCs" with larger screens that are used in hospitals by surgeons and in other work environments such as factories.

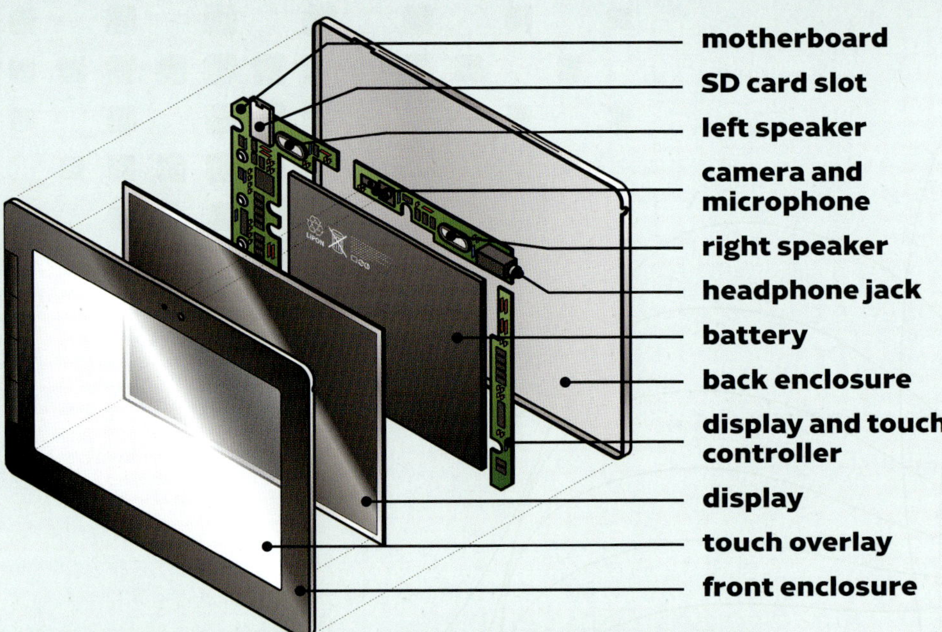

Touch screen tablets are designed to be as thin as possible, while remaining rigid and tough. Each of the major components are constructed as flat layers.

How Are Touch Screens Made?

You may use touch screen technology every day but have you ever wondered what goes into building touch screens? The main building blocks of all touch screen devices are the display, which you touch to control the device; the sensor system, which detects any contact on the display; and the driver software, which is the computer program that tells a computer in the device what the screen is, how to respond to touches, and how to display results.

Made of Many Layers

In most touch screens, the display is a flat screen made from glass or a type of hard plastic called polyester. Usually, the underside of the plastic screen is coated with a very thin metallic layer. The base of the display consists of another glass or plastic screen. The top of this screen is coated with the same clear metallic layer.

The heaviest part of any tablet is the internal battery, which is also thin and flat. The main processor on the motherboard and the color display use most of the power supply.

Creating a Gap

The two screens press together to form a sandwich, but the two metallic layers are held apart using sticky spacers. The gap between the layers is very thin. The two metallic layers touch only when the screen is pressed with a stylus or a person's finger. This sends a message to the touch screen driver.

In most cases, fixing a smartphone or replacing the touch screen or battery requires an expert.

Perfect for Touch Screens

The metallic layers in most touch screens consist of a rare metal called indium, which is mixed with oxygen and another metal called tin. Like all metals, indium is a conductor. However, the indium compound is unusual because it is transparent. This makes it perfect for touch screen use.

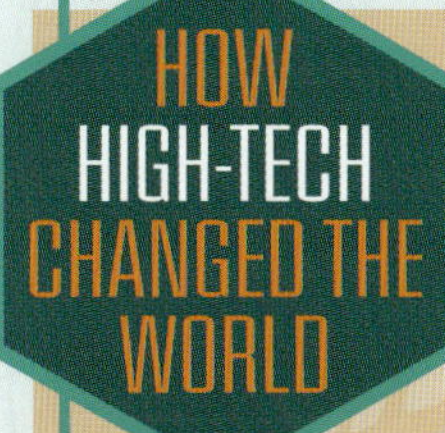

You probably know someone who has dropped their smartphone and it has resulted in a cracked touch screen. Today, a dropped phone is far less likely to crack than early smartphones. This is largely due to Gorilla Glass. Invented by technology company Corning, Gorilla Glass is strengthened with chemicals and is the result of decades of scientific research. Launched in 2007 with the first iPhone, it is designed to be light, thin, and resistant to cracks. The latest version of Gorilla Glass can be found on smart watches, televisions, and tablets, as well as smartphones.

CHAPTER 3

USING TOUCH SCREENS

Ergonomics is the science of making machines easier for people to use. Touch screens use ergonomics to improve the way people work with computers, smartphones, video games, and other electronic equipment. Before touch screens, most people pressed buttons or used a mouse and keyboard to control computers and other electronic equipment. Today, you can control the same equipment using your fingers, a stylus, or a digital pen.

No Need for a Mouse

Resistive touch screens work as long as the two metallic layers in the glass display make contact. This means you can use your fingers, a stylus, or pen to press on the display. The screen registers the touching point when the metal layers touch. SAW, infrared, and optical touch screens can also be operated using almost any type of input to register a touch on the screen.

Touch screen technology, used with a stylus, allows people to draw on specialized pads that accurately measure the pressure and even the angle of the stylus.

Capacitive touch screens do have some drawbacks. One problem is the thin film of skin oil that smears the screen as you rub your finger across it. Many touch screens now include an oil-resistant coating.

Using Your Fingers

Capacitive touch screens are different. These devices rely on the human body to conduct some of the electrical charge away from the screen. Capacitive touch screens will work only when you use your fingers to control them. One of the main advantages of capacitive touch screens is ergonomics. Users feel they can connect with the devices directly, so they are often easier to use and seem more responsive.

HOW HIGH-TECH CHANGED THE WORLD

The manufacturers of devices spend many millions of dollars to constantly improve the ergonomics of their touch screens. The accuracy and sensitivity to touch are just two of the most-obvious qualities. The size of the buttons on the screen need to be the right size to hit with a fingertip, and the user should be able to customize their layout. Touch feedback, such as a short vibrating buzz, can also be built in. Today, screen readers with voice control are common features that allow people with physical disabilities to use touch screens more easily.

Modern multitouch screen phones support complex games that require superfast responses.

More than One Finger

Many modern touch screens allow people to use more than one finger at a time to control computers and other electronic equipment. These screens are called multitouch screens, and they are changing the way people interact with these devices.

The Multitouch Story

Multitouch research began in the early 1980s at the University of Toronto in Canada. Scientists there built a touch screen that consisted of a frosted glass panel with a camera behind it. The researchers used one or more fingers to move over the screen. Each finger touch showed up on the camera as a dark spot, which registered as a command on the computer connected to the screen.

News of a New Technology

The next step in the development of multitouch screens came in the 1990s, when a group of scientists published a report on the new technology. They described a touch screen that could be controlled with taps, swipes, and even a "virtual" touch screen keyboard.

Today's Multitouch Screens

Several companies have tried to develop multitouch screens. Apple led the way with their high-tech smartphone, called the iPhone. The first iPhone was released in 2007. Three years later, the company released its multitouch tablet computer: the iPad. Apple's iPhone and iPad are controlled using specific finger movements. They include "pinching" the screen with the thumb and index finger to zoom out on the display and "spreading" the screen in the opposite direction to zoom in. These movements are called multitouch gestures.

HOW HIGH-TECH CHANGED THE WORLD

Recent years have seen a demand in the rise of the smart watch. These have a color touch screen and many functions of a smartphone, but their screens are small as they have to fit on your wrist. To make them easier to use, smart watches use custom gestures. The user creates their own gestures in an app and links it to a command. This way you can make the watch open an app, such as a map, just by drawing an "m" shape with a fingertip on its touch screen.

Many smart watch apps and features are shown as clear icons that can be easily pressed.

Touch screens make access to information easier for everyone, including people who may be less used to technology.

Advantages Are Everything

Touch screen devices are replacing personal computers and other electronic equipment that rely on a keyboard, buttons, or a mouse. There are many advantages to using touch screen control. For a start, touch screen technology is easy to use—the user simply points at what they want to select. For many people, being able to touch or tap a screen is more natural than using a keyboard and a computer mouse. Touch screen technology makes devices faster and more ergonomic (see pages 22–23). Young children and older people in particular, who do not use computers very often, can quickly learn how to use different touch screen devices.

Made for Everyone

A touch screen displays all the options, guiding the user through each step. This makes touch screens perfect for first-time use, for example, in a kiosk (see pages 28–29). People who have disabilities may find it very difficult to use both a keyboard and mouse, so touch screens are an easier and more accessible technology for them.

Tough and Reliable

A touch screen is tougher and more reliable than a keyboard and mouse. This makes them ideal for use in public areas, such as libraries. The glass display is easy to clean and can be coated in special layers to prevent damage by dust and grease.

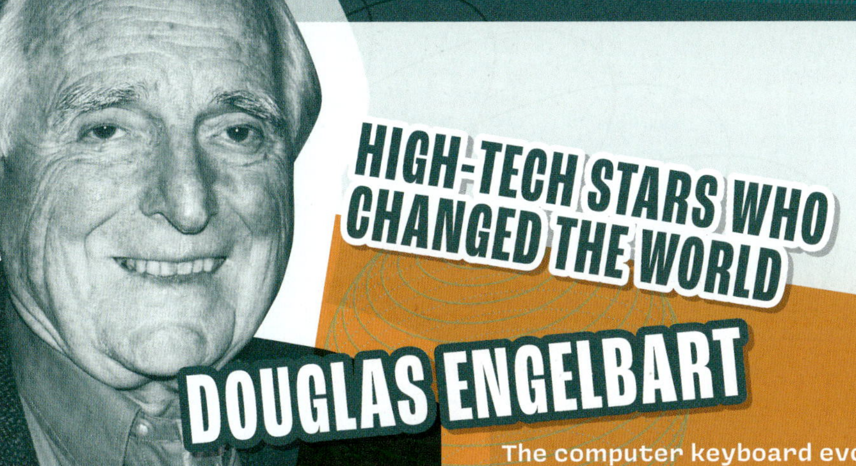

HIGH-TECH STARS WHO CHANGED THE WORLD

DOUGLAS ENGELBART

The computer keyboard evolved from the typewriter. However, keyboards lack an easy and intuitive way of moving a cursor and selecting options. This was made possible with the invention of the computer mouse, which is the ancestor of the touch screen. The first mouse was created by engineer and inventor Douglas Engelbart (1925–2013) in the mid-1960s. It was made from wood and had two internal wheels that detected motion when the device moved over a surface. Engelbart's team called it a mouse, because its connection cable resembled a tail. The invention of the mouse made using a computer much simpler, thereby making computers much more accessible to nonexperts.

Touch screen devices save space because there is no need for a monitor, keyboard, mouse, and cables. They are also easily portable, so you can easily take your work anywhere.

CHAPTER 4

TOUCH SCREENS ARE EVERYWHERE

Touch screens have many uses in our lives. Many people now use touch screen devices such as smartphones, sat-nav units, and tablet computers. Some people use touch screen technology without even realizing it.

Making Sales Simple

One of the first consumer uses for touch screens was for cash registers. The first one was developed in 1986 and worked with an early Atari computer. At the time, this was cutting-edge technology. Today, touch screen cash registers are common. They make the sales process quick and easy for the customer and the sales assistant.

Touch Screens in Kiosks

Self-service kiosks are one of the most popular uses for touch screen technology. These interactive devices provide 24-hour customer service because they do not rely on a member of staff to serve the customer. Touch screen kiosks are user-friendly. They provide the user with choices at each step, guiding them through the sales process. Many people now use touch screen technology to purchase tickets at movie theaters and bus and railroad stations.

Many cafés now use touch screens to record both orders and transactions.

Cash Withdrawal at a Touch

Another common consumer use for touch screen technology is ATMs. People use ATMs to check their bank balance and withdraw cash by tapping on a series of icons on the screen. Touch screens are ideal for this purpose because they are easy for people to work and can withstand repeated and heavy use.

Drawing the User In

Touch screen advertising panels encourage people to find out about products by engaging with the display. They can prompt the user to play games and complete surveys, which help companies learn more about the people to whom they wish to sell their products.

HOW HIGH-TECH CHANGED THE WORLD

In the mid-2010s, fast food giant McDonald's began introducing touch screens in their restaurants. They let people choose food and drink from a menu, order it, and pay on the spot. The idea was that ordering food would become a more "fun" activity for younger people who were used to computers and other devices. The touch screens increased profits for McDonald's because they allowed diners to take more time customizing their order, often by adding optional extras and so increasing how much they spent. Today, most fast food restaurants use touch screen technology for ordering food both in the store and at drive-throughs.

Touch Screens in the Workplace

Computer touch screens are perhaps the most common use of touch screen technology in the workplace. However, there are many other applications in other industries, ranging from medicine to manufacturing.

Keeping Things Efficient

Touch screens are common in the workplace because they are so easy to use. They allow people to do their jobs quickly and more efficiently with fewer mistakes and less training. Touch screens can withstand heavy use, and they are easy to clean and maintain.

Touch Screens in Healthcare

Touch screens are used in a lot of medical equipment. For example, surgeons use interactive touch screens to explore images of the inside of a patient's body to help them perform complex surgery. Doctors can also carry a portable touch screen device with their patients' records, making hospital rounds more efficient. Patients also use touch computers (see page 38–39) to fill out their medical information and surveys that help doctors diagnose illnesses.

Today, doctors may use touch screen devices to share the results of medical examinations with patients.

Factories can be dangerous places. By using wireless touch screen controllers factory workers can keep a safe distance from hazardous machinery and can even perform diagnostic tests to identify faults remotely.

Useful in Transportation

Touch screens are often built into modern car designs. By using the touch screen, drivers can control a linked smartphone, their music, and the sat-nav equipment used to find their way around. Since they are easy to use, touch screens can be operated while on the move. Pilots also rely on sat-nav touch screen technology to keep airplanes on course during flights.

Found in Factories

Factories often use touch screens to help automate manufacturing. Before touch screens, workers used machines with many buttons, knobs, and switches. It took a long time to learn how to use these complex machines. Today, touch screen displays make the process much easier and a lot quicker.

HOW HIGH-TECH CHANGED THE WORLD

Touch screens have also revolutionized the design of airplane cockpits. Traditionally, cockpits had hundreds of buttons and switches necessary for pilots to do their job. Because modern jet airliners are relying more and more on computers for a stable flight, touch screens can be used so that pilots can interact with them, without introducing more and more buttons and switches to the cockpit. They can automatically change what they display when the airplane is taking off or landing. They also include safety features so that an accidental touch during turbulence is not interpreted as a command.

Fun at the Touch of a Screen

Touch screens are ideal for game consoles. They make gaming interactive and games easy to play. Handheld touch screen game consoles are now common. Many people also like to download apps and play games on tablets, smartphones, and touch computers. These devices offer high-definition and interactive gaming at a fraction of the cost of traditional consoles such as the PlayStation 5 and Microsoft Xbox series.

Around 40 percent of all app downloads on smartphones and tablets are games.

Touch Screens in Gaming

The Japanese company Sega tried to build a touch screen control for a game console in the 1990s. This early attempt did not succeed because touch screen technology was too expensive. It took another ten years before touch screen gaming became a reality.

Nintendo Success

The Nintendo DS was a handheld game console that included touch screen control using a stylus. This device was released for sale in 2004, and has since sold more than 150 million units. The Nintendo DS works using a resistive touch screen. By putting pressure on the screen, users can control the gaming action.

Used in Amusement Arcades

Touch screens are also common in the video games found in amusement arcades. Arcade games' touch screens can be small or large, and they are made from tough glass to withstand heavy use. Touch screens are easy to use, so anyone can use the controls to play these games.

Touch screen arcade games provide a more immersive gaming experience.

HIGH-TECH HISTORY

The very first handheld games console to feature a touchscreen was the Game.com. It was launched in 1997 and was also the first handheld console that could connect to the Internet. Its screen was just 2.5 inches (6.3 cm) across and was black and white, rather than color. The touch screen was not very precise, so a grid of 12 by 10 squares was printed on the screen itself, showing where to press with the stylus. However, the console's lack of color or illumination for its screen meant it was not very successful.

All about Phones

Smartphones made the touch screen an everyday item. Before touch screens, people pressed tiny buttons to make calls, send messages, and surf the World Wide Web (WWW). Today, many smartphones work by touching and interacting with icons on the screen.

The First Touch Screen Phone

The first touch screen cell phone, IBM's Simon Personal Communicator, came onto the market in 1994. The phone combined the features of a personal digital assistant (PDA)—such as messaging and a calendar—with voice calls. The Ericsson R380 was the first touch screen cell phone to be sold as a "smartphone." It also combined the functions of a PDA and cell phone. It worked much like a computer, using an operating system called Symbian.

Apple Takes Over

Apple revolutionized touch screen technology in 2007, with the release of the iPhone. This device included a large capacitive touch screen. It allowed people to interact with the iPhone using multitouch finger control (see pages 24–25). Every time you touch the iPhone's screen, it sends electrical signals to the phone's microprocessor. The processor is the iPhone's "brain" and tells the device what to do. For example, it converts a finger "spread" into a command that the processor recognizes to zoom in on the screen.

A touch screen lets you use editing apps to easily alter your photos before sharing them.

People lined up to buy the brand new iPhone X in 2017, which featured facial recognition for the first time.

Something New Each Time

Apple has released many versions of the iPhone. Each version has come with new features, such as fingerprint recognition, improved cameras with face recognition, and voice control. Users can also choose from thousands of different apps to add new features to their phones.

HIGH-TECH HISTORY

In 2005, the search engine company Google bought another company, Android Inc., for at least $50 million. Over the next few years Google used its expensive purchase to develop a mobile operating system to compete with Apple, which used its own iOS operating system in its devices. Android was unveiled in 2008, and is used on all of Google's own touch screen phones, watches, and tablets, as well as those made by other companies, such as Samsung. Android has overtaken iOS in popularity and, by 2023 had more than twice as many users worldwide than iOS.

Touch Screen Tablets

Tablet computers are all-in-one mobile computers that do not use a normal keyboard and mouse for control. They rely on large touch screens, finger or stylus control, and a virtual keyboard.

Early Tablets

Intel introduced the WebPAD or Intel Web Tablet in 1999, but scrapped the project before it could be launched. Two years later, Microsoft Corporation developed special software to run tablet computers. Early tablets running on Microsoft software had resistive touch screens and needed a stylus or pen for control. Virtual keyboards did not exist at the time, so many early tablets also included a removable keyboard.

Developing the Screens

The design of modern tablets has followed in the footsteps of touch screen smartphones. They combine the processing power of a normal PC with the smartphone's ease of use. They use capacitive touch screens with multitouch finger control and virtual keyboards to make them easy to use. These new tablets represent a new type of computing that can be easily carried out when on the move.

Tablets made by Google and Apple use operating systems that are more advanced versions of the systems used by smartphones. This makes it easy for people to install the same apps on both types of device.

The most popular tablet computer is Apple's iPad—released in 2010. The iPad put tablet computing firmly on the map. Other tablets soon followed, including Amazon's Kindle Fire and Samsung's Galaxy Tab, among others.

Writing Versus Typing

Some modern tablets still use a stylus for control. Some include handwriting recognition software instead of a keyboard. This involves writing on the surface of the screen with a digital pen. The tablet converts the writing into text on the screen. Handwriting recognition software has been around for a long time. It is not very accurate, however, and most people prefer to type using a physical or virtual keyboard.

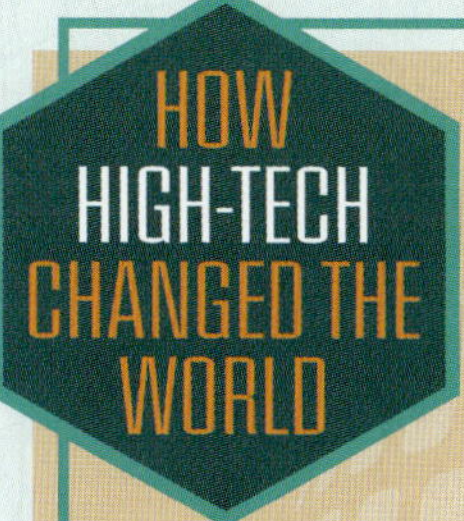

In 2007, Amazon launched its Kindle tablet. It had a type of screen known as E Ink, designed especially for making on-screen text easy to read. Amazon began as an online book store and the Kindle was aimed at people who preferred their books in digital form. Later generations of the Kindle included the ability to download books wirelessly and touch screens. The Kindle Scribe, launched in 2022, even allows users to write on the E Ink display using a stylus, so people can add notes while reading a book.

Combining Old and New Tech

Modern computing has come full circle with the development of touch computers. These computers are conventional desktop PCs that have interactive touch screen monitors. Touch computers are normal desktop PCs that combine a multitouch monitor with a keyboard and mouse. Touch computers grew out of the popularity of smartphones and tablets. However, touch computers have a further advantage—the processing power of a normal computer.

Adding Touch

Some touch computers are all-in-one touch screen PCs. All the computer parts, such as the processor and memory, are built into the same housing as the touch screen display. You can also buy a touch screen display and connect it to your existing computer. All you need to do is update your computer with the latest multitouch software to take advantage of the latest touch screen technology.

Microsoft Success

Microsoft Corporation has inbuilt multitouch technology in its operating systems—the computer programs that control how the computer works. Microsoft's latest operating system—Windows 11—comes with a range of new features. For example, most multitouch systems work with two-finger control. Windows 11 supports apps that work with up to five fingers, making them much more interactive.

A mouse can be connected to a touch computer if desired but the combination of touch screen and keyboard is popular with many users.

The ability to draw directly on to a screen is a very fast and easy way to amend and edit files.

Making a Connection

Multitouch monitors come with two cables to connect to a PC—a standard monitor cable and a USB cable to enable the touch screen functions. You can buy a touch screen monitor and connect it to a standard PC in this way. Once it is connected, and the right drivers installed, you will have a touch screen computer!

HIGH-TECH HISTORY

Before the iPad or smartphones, people who wanted the latest technology could buy a PDA. These are handheld computers that handle files, contacts, and other basic functions. The earliest models relied on a miniature keyboard but in 1993, Apple released the first one that had a touch screen capable of recognizing handwriting. This function worked so poorly it even became a joke in an episode of the television show *The Simpsons*. However, the Apple Newton did prove that people wanted more advanced touch screens in their devices.

CHAPTER 5

LEADING THE WAY WITH TECH

Touch screen technology has come a long way in a short time. Some exciting developments in computing include gesture control to allow people to use computers without touching them at all! Another new development is tactile touch screens, which rely on a technology called haptics.

Using Gestures

A current area of development in touch screen technology is gesture control, which extends the idea of touch screen technology. Researchers hope to build computers that do not require any mechanical controls, so instead of swiping or tapping on a screen, you might be able to control a computer by simply clicking your fingers, flicking your wrist, or pointing at the display. Computers can already recognize facial expressions, body language, and complex hand gestures such as sign language.

Many controllers for gaming consoles include a buzzing function to register types of physical contact in a game.

"Gorilla arm" is a side effect of using a touch screen device for too long, especially when holding the device vertically: the user's arm begins to ache and feel tired. Some people think that this might lead to the downfall of touch screen technology.

All-New Game Control

Game consoles such as the PlayStation 5 are leading the way with gesture control. These devices use motion sensor technology to control the action on the screen. The PlayStation 5's controller works using an accelerometer. This device measures the way the player's hand moves while they play a game. The accelerometer feeds this information back to a sensor mounted on the display, which recreates the movements on the screen. Microsoft's Kinect system works using an infrared sensor and camera to track the movement of people playing a game. Kinect also uses speech recognition so people can control the game with their voice.

HOW HIGH-TECH CHANGED THE WORLD

In 2012, the Leap Motion controller was released by Leap Motion Inc. It is a small device that sits on a surface and points two infrared cameras up at the space above it. It can track hands moving above it to an accuracy of less than 0.04 inches (1 mm). Having two cameras gives the controller stereo vision so it can track hands in 3-D. Apps developed for the Leap Motion include virtual chess, virtual piano, and other games, all of which can be used without touching a screen or a keyboard.

Trainee airline pilots are taught in flight simulation settings, with screens that connect to controls to mimic what flying a plane in real life looks and feels like.

Using the Tech

Many new developments may result from the boom in touch screen technology. Touch screens of the future may offer even more new and exciting ways for people to interact with their computers.

Texture on the Screen

One exciting development includes tactile touch screens that create different textures on the surface of the screen. For example, touch screens of the future could recreate the feel of objects they display. So, you might feel the texture of fur by touching an image of an animal on the screen.

Feeling an Action

As far-fetched as feeling textures on a screen may sound, researchers are developing this idea with a technology called haptics. In fact, this technology already exists in flight simulators and video games, where the controller vibrates to feel exactly like action on the screen. Engineers have also used haptic technology to design tactile "buttons" on touch screen devices such as smartphones and tablet computers, which will make using the devices a far more sensory experience for people.

Learning about the High-Tech

One of the most important applications of haptic technology is within education and training. Research has shown that the sense of touch is very powerful. People respond better to learning when they can interact with and touch the objects they are learning about.

Bend and Flex

Another new touch screen development is the idea of flexible touch screens that act like a sheet of paper and can bend around corners. This idea could be used to develop electronic devices that people can wear, such as touch screen watch straps or clothing.

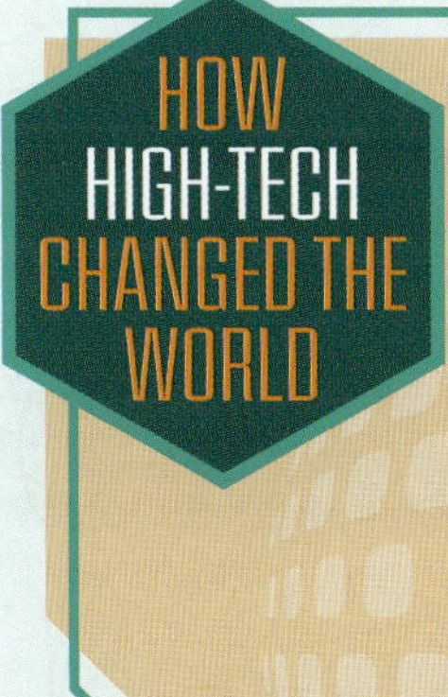

The first smartphone that came with a flexible screen was the Royole FlexPal, which was launched in 2018. The following year Samsung released the Galaxy Fold, which is a smartphone that the user can fold open horizontally to reveal a single continuous touch screen. It is designed to be durable—users can expect to be able to open up the folding screen around 200,000 times before the fold fails. This is equivalent to around five years of normal use.

The success of touch screens is driving a demand for ever-more sophisticated technology.

CONCLUSION

A HIGH-TECH FUTURE

A few decades ago, touch screen technology was found mostly in science-fiction books and movies. Today, it is difficult to imagine a world without touch screens. They are everywhere—in our homes, banks, stores, and restaurants, cars and airplanes, and in the workplace.

Tech for Everyone

The first touch screens were expensive. Scientists invented and used the devices for special electronic equipment in big research laboratories. Over time, the cost of touch screens fell. Today, many everyday electronic gadgets have touch screens to control them, from smartphones, smart watches, and tablets to game consoles.

Changing People's Relationship with Tech

Touch screen technology has really changed the way people interact with electronic devices. Most people find it easier to point at an icon on a screen than to use a keyboard and mouse. Touching a screen feels more natural to people and makes these devices easier to use.

Touch screens have a long history of scientific research and invention but it is their use in personal devices that has made them familiar to us all.

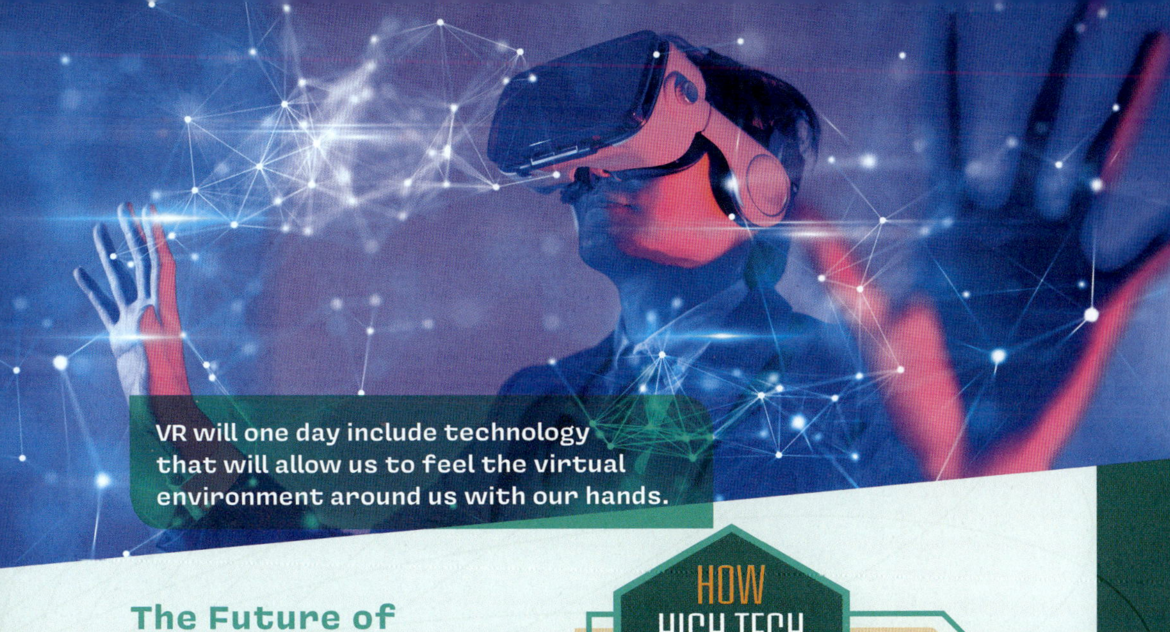

VR will one day include technology that will allow us to feel the virtual environment around us with our hands.

The Future of Touch Tech

Touch screen technology has moved quickly in the last ten years. What does the future hold for the touch screens of tomorrow? Scientists have already developed tactile touch screens. These high-tech devices have screens that mimic different textures, such as rough and smooth. Future touch screens may also combine with other technologies, such as virtual reality (VR), to make electronic gadgets even more interactive.

A Virtual World

In the future, people may use senses other than touch to engage with computers and other electronic equipment. For example, you might use these devices in a "virtual world," using eyeglasses and sensors in your clothes to interact and control what you see.

HOW HIGH-TECH CHANGED THE WORLD

Augmented reality (AR) adds virtual objects into the real world through smartphones or wearable technology called AR glasses. These use a tiny projector to put digital information on to the inside of a glass lens so that the wearer can see a head-up display that is relevant to their real-world surroundings. Eye tracking technology for PCs already exists, allowing users to move and click a cursor just by moving their eyes and blinking. Future AR glasses will incorporate eye tracking, making it possible to easily navigate the large amount of potential digital information they can display.

GLOSSARY

accelerometer a device that measures acceleration (the rate of increase of speed over time)

atoms tiny particles that make up matter

cathode-ray tube a device in televisions and computer terminals that sends an image onto the screen

driver software a computer program that allows different electronic devices to "speak" to one another

electricity energy that arises from the movement of charged particles

electronic circuits networks of electronic parts connected by conductors

ergonomics the science of making machines easier for people to use

filament a very thin piece or thread of wire inside a lightbulb

gesture control controlling a machine with movements or facial expressions

haptics technology that involves the control of machines through touch

hard drive part of an electronic device that stores information

icon a small picture on a screen that allows people to interact with computers and other equipment

infrared light a form of light energy with a slightly longer wavelength than the visible light we can see

input device equipment used to put data into a computer

Internet the worldwide network of computers that provides email and web pages

light-emitting diode (LED) a tiny device used in electronics as a light source

microprocessor a device that processes all the information in an electronic device such as a computer

miniaturization making something smaller

operating system a computer program that controls how a computer works

particle accelerator a machine that accelerates atoms and other tiny particles to very high speeds

patents legal documents that protect inventors' ideas

pixels the smallest area on a computer screen that can be given a separate colour by the computer

polyester clear, hard plastic sometimes used to make the outer covering of a touch screen

reflector material that reflects light

satellite navigation system (sat-nav) a system that uses a series of satellites in orbit around Earth to map the location of objects on the surface of the planet

smartphones cell phones that have some of the features of personal computers

stylus a penlike instrument that can be used to control some touch screen devices

tablets small, portable computers contained within flat screens

transducer an electronic device that changes energy from one form into another

virtual keyboard a keyboard that appears on the touch screen and is used to enter information

FIND OUT MORE

Books

Crest, Mason. *Gadgets and Devices* (Science & Technology). Mason Crest Publishers, 2019.

Mason, Paul. *Jobs in Technology* (The Best Ever Jobs). PowerKids Press, 2022.

Musolf, Nell. *Google* (Odysseys in Business). Creative Education, 2024.

Rea, Amy C. *Computer Technology* (Milestones in Technology). Child's World, 2023.

Websites

What makes tablets work? Find out at:
https://electronics.howstuffworks.com/gadgets/high-tech-gadgets/ipad.htm

Discover more about touch screens, from their history to applications at:
https://kids.kiddle.co/Touchscreen

Find out what happened on January 9, 2007, when Steve Jobs introduced the iPhone at:
https://www.history.com/this-day-in-history/steve-jobs-debuts-the-iphone

Publisher's note to educators and parents:
All the websites featured above have been carefully reviewed to ensure that they are suitable for students. However, many websites change often, and we cannot guarantee that a site's future contents will continue to meet our high standards of educational value. Please be advised that students should be closely monitored whenever they access the Internet.

INDEX

ABOUT THE AUTHOR

Kelly Roberts has written many children's science and technology books. In writing and researching this book, she has learned just how much touch screen technology has changed our daily lives.